The Ancient Civilizations of
Greece and Rome

Solving Algebraic Equations

Kerri O'Donnell

PowerMath™

The Rosen Publishing Group's
PowerKids Press™
New York

Published in 2005 by The Rosen Publishing Group, Inc.
29 East 21st Street, New York, NY 10010

Book Design: Haley Wilson

Photo Credits: Cover © Massimo Mastrorillo/Corbis; p. 5 (Greek Temple) © Roger Wood/Corbis; p. 5 (Roman Forum) © ML Sinibaldi/Corbis; p. 7 © Gustavo Tomsich/Corbis; pp. 8, 11 © Archivo Iconografico, S.A./Corbis; p. 9 © Wolfgang Kaehler/Corbis; p. 15 © James Davis; Eye Ubiquitous/Corbis; p. 17 © Mimmo Jodice/Corbis; p. 19 © Jose Fuste Raga/Corbis; p. 21 © Gianni Dagli Orti/Corbis; p. 23 © Bettmann/Corbis; p. 25 © Araldo de Luca/Corbis; pp. 26–27 © John Heseltine/Corbis; p. 29 © Jim Sugar/Corbis; p. 30 © Joseph Sohm; ChromoSohm Inc./Corbis.

Library of Congress Cataloging-in-Publication Data

O'Donnell, Kerri, 1972-
  The ancient civilizations of Greece and Rome : solving algebraic equations / Kerri O'Donnell.
      p. cm. — (PowerMath)
  Includes index.
  ISBN 1-4042-2930-2 (library binding)
  ISBN 1-4042-5123-5 (pbk.)
  6-pack ISBN 1-4042-5124-3
  1. Equations—Numerical solutions—Juvenile literature. 2. Civilization, Classical—Juvenile literature. I.
Title. II. Series.
  QA218.O46 2005
  512.9'4—dc22

                              2004007066

Manufactured in the United States of America

Contents

Ancient Greece and Rome

The term "ancient civilization" refers to a society that existed long ago. It is often used to describe societies that developed around the Mediterranean Sea starting around 3000 B.C. and ending in A.D. 476 with the fall of the Roman Empire.

The civilizations of Greece and Rome were 2 of many civilizations that flourished around the Mediterranean Sea region during this period. They are often discussed together because of the great influence the culture of ancient Greece had on the later culture of ancient Rome.

Ancient Greece reached its peak about 2,500 years ago and is often called the "birthplace of Western civilization." Many of our modern ideas about science, **philosophy,** government, and art are based on the work of ancient Greeks. Ancient Rome reached its peak over 1,900 years ago. Its culture borrowed heavily from ancient Greek culture. Because the Roman Empire grew so large and lasted for many centuries, it also had a great influence on Western civilization.

In this book, we will use algebra, a branch of mathematics that is an extension of basic arithmetic operations. By forming algebraic **equations** that use letters to represent unknown numbers, we will solve math problems about these two great civilizations.

Greek temple

Ancient Greece's influence can be seen in much of the architecture of ancient Rome. The Forum in Rome—the center of government during the Roman Empire—borrowed from Greek temples like the one shown above.

Roman Forum

5

A Closer Look at Ancient Greece

Ancient Greek civilization can be traced back to the Minoan (muh-NOH-uhn) civilization that developed about 3000 B.C. on the island of Crete. Crete is located south of modern-day Greece in the Aegean Sea. This civilization was named for King Minos, the legendary ruler of Greece. The Minoans were skilled sailors and traders. **Archaeologists** have found remains of the Minoans' great palaces. The **architecture** shows they were a wealthy people with great building skills. Inscriptions show they had their own writing system.

By about 1600 B.C., small villages were established on the Greek mainland by people from the north. By about 1450 B.C., these villages had grown into larger towns built around palaces. This is called the Mycenaean (my-suh-NEE-uhn) culture, named after the powerful town of Mycenae (my-SEE-nee) in southern Greece.

The Minoans controlled most of the area around the Aegean Sea until about 1450 B.C. They were eventually overpowered by the Mycenaeans, who borrowed many ideas from the Minoan culture.

Let's say that in 1450 B.C. there were 48 villages in a certain region, 17 under Minoan control and the rest controlled by Mycenae. We could use simple subtraction to find out how many villages were controlled by Mycenae.

48	total villages in a region
−17	villages under Minoan control
31	villages controlled by Mycenae

The Minoans were skilled artists. The dolphins shown here are part of a fresco found at a Minoan palace in Crete.

We were able to solve the problem on page 6 by using subtraction. We can also use algebra to solve this problem. Algebra is a kind of mathematics that can help us find answers quickly and easily. It uses both numbers and symbols in standard math operations. The numbers in algebra problems are called **constants** because their value doesn't change. For example, 48 is always 48. It never represents 47 or 49 or any other number. Algebra problems also have **variables**. The variables are represented by letters and stand for unknown numbers whose values can vary.

royal Greek
death mask

Let's use the information on page 6 to rewrite the math problem as an algebraic equation.

$$x \text{ (variable)} + 17 \text{ (constant)} = 48 \text{ (constant)}$$

To find the value of x, you must change the form of the equation so that x is alone on the left side. Whatever you have on the right side will be the value of x. You can get x alone by subtracting 17 from the left side of the equation. When you subtract 17 from the left side, you must also subtract 17 from the right side to keep both sides equal.

$$x + 17 = 48$$
$$x + 17 - 17 = 48 - 17$$
$$x = 31$$

Mycenae controlled 31 villages.

Ancient royal graves at Mycenae contained jewels, weapons, and objects made of bronze, silver, and gold. Royalty were often buried with "death masks" like the object shown on page 8. On this page is a crown made of gold.

gold crown

From a Dark Age to a Golden Age

By about 1250 B.C., Mycenaean civilization had begun to break apart. A period known as a dark age—a time of wars and invasions—began on the Greek mainland and lasted until about 800 B.C.

During the dark age, people lived in small tribal villages, there was a decline in the arts and architecture, commerce deteriorated, and writing systems were abandoned. Stories from the past were preserved orally through songs and poetry. Some of these oral narratives were written down around the end of the dark age, most notably the *Iliad* and the *Odyssey*. Today, these narratives that dealt with historical, legendary, or mythical events are called epic poems.

When the dark age ended, the Greeks began to use a writing system based on the Phoenician (fih-NEE-shun) alphabet. The Phoenicians were a people who lived along the Mediterranean Sea. The Greeks began trading with them when commerce was revived.

Greeks traded things they had—like olive oil—for things they needed—like grain, wood, and glassware. Let's say a Greek trader gave a Phoenician trader 2 times as many jars of olive oil as the number of glasses the Phoenician trader gave him in return. If we know that the Greek trader gave the Phoenician trader 240 jars of olive oil, we can figure out how many glasses he received. Let's look at page 11 to see how we'd set this up as an algebraic equation.

We know that the Greek trader gave the Phoenician trader 2 times as many jars of olive oil as the number of glasses he received.

x = number of glasses

$2x$ = 240 (jars of olive oil)

Now, we must divide both sides of the equation by 2:

$$\frac{2x}{2} = \frac{240}{2}$$

$$x = 120$$

The Greek trader received 120 glasses for the olive oil.

Greece's war with Troy was the subject of an epic poem called the *Iliad*. The *Iliad* is one of the most famous works of Greek literature. It is thought to have been composed by a blind poet named Homer around 800 B.C. This painting shows what a Renaissance artist imagined Homer looked like.

Around 1250 B.C., city-states—regions whose politics and culture were organized around a single town or city—were established. Early Greek city-states were ruled by kings, then by wealthy citizens. City-states fought each other for land, and some—like Sparta and Athens—grew large and powerful. From the 700s B.C. to the 500s B.C., the Greeks established large city-states around the Mediterranean.

The farmers and merchants in Greece's city-states were free men who wanted to participate in the government. The wealthy leaders refused and the people revolted. Many city-states began to develop democratic governments. In 508 B.C., the ruler of Athens introduced changes that allowed all free men to vote in Athens's **assembly**. Let's say the total number of merchants and farmers in the assembly was 108. If we know that there were 43 farmers in the assembly, let's use algebra to find out how many merchants were in the assembly.

Remember: you must do the same operation to both sides of the equation.

x = number of merchants in the Athenian assembly

43 = number of farmers in the Athenian assembly

108 = total number of merchants and farmers in the assembly

$$x + 43 = 108$$
$$x + 43 - 43 = 108 - 43$$
$$x = 65$$

There were 65 merchants in the Athenian assembly.

During this time, the Persian (PUHR-zhun) empire was growing and had taken over many Greek city-states in Asia Minor, which is now Turkey. "Persia" was the ancient name for the area in southwestern Asia that is now known as Iran. Greek city-states put aside their differences and joined to defeat the Persians in 479 B.C.

The peace between Athens and Sparta did not last long after the Persians were defeated. Athens joined with city-states in the Aegean islands and Asia Minor and developed a powerful navy. Sparta joined with city-states in the southern part of the Greek mainland and formed a powerful army.

While Athens and Sparta battled for control of the Greek world during the 400s B.C., Greece experienced its "Golden Age," which lasted from 477 B.C. to 431 B.C. During this time, Athens became Greece's main cultural center and grew in power and wealth. Greek writers wrote many famous dramas that are still read and performed today. In fact, drama had its beginning in ancient Greece. The Greeks held singing and dancing festivals as early as the 600s B.C., then later held drama festivals to honor their gods.

Much of Greece's most famous architecture and sculpture was created during Greece's Golden Age. A temple called the Parthenon is perhaps the most famous example of Greek architecture that still survives today. The rectangular Parthenon was built on Athens's **acropolis** between 447 B.C. and 432 B.C. It measures about 237 feet long by 60 feet high. If its width is 50 feet more than its height, how many feet wide is it? We can set this up as an algebraic equation.

x = **width of Parthenon**
x = **height + 50**
x = **60 + 50**
x = **110**

The Parthenon is 110 feet wide.

The Parthenon was made of white marble that was brought to Athens from a mountain 11 miles away. It is surrounded by 46 columns and has a large central space divided into 2 rooms.

The End of the Golden Age

Greece's Golden Age came to an end in 431 B.C. with the start of the Peloponnesian (peh-luh-puh-NEE-zhun) War. This war between rival city-states Athens and Sparta lasted for about 27 years. Shortly after the war began, Athens was struck by a **plague** that killed many of its people, including some of its leaders. Athens surrendered to Sparta in 404 B.C. Sparta controlled the Greek world for only a few years before fighting broke out once again between various Greek city-states.

In 338 B.C., Greece was conquered by a country to the north named Macedonia (ma-suh-DOH-nee-uh). A few years later, Alexander the Great of Macedonia conquered the Persian empire. His empire now stretched from Greece to India, and Greek culture and ideas traveled farther east as the empire spread.

Greece remained part of Macedonia until about 146 B.C., when the region was taken over by the Romans. Although Greece's city-states were no longer strong political or military powers, their economy grew stronger under Roman rule and they once again created great art and pursued learning. The Romans took what they learned from Greek culture and spread Greek ideas throughout their lands.

This image of Alexander the Great is from a Roman mosaic done in the 100s B.C., long after Alexander's death.

A Village Becomes an Empire

Rome was founded in 753 B.C. on the Tiber River in central Italy. At that time, Rome was just a small village, but it would eventually become the center of one of the largest and most powerful empires in the history of the world.

The first Romans were farmers and shepherds who planted and harvested their crops for most of the year, then served in the army during the summer months. As more and more people came from surrounding lands to settle on the Italian **peninsula**, Rome's army grew larger, and Rome became more and more powerful. In 509 B.C., the Roman **Republic** was established. Let's say that in 509 B.C., the number of Roman men in a certain region was 2,485. Let's also say that 1,355 of these men were soldiers in Rome's army. We can use an algebraic equation to find out how many men were not in the army.

$$x + 1,355 = 2,485$$
$$x + 1,355 - 1,355 = 2,485 - 1,355$$
$$x = 1,130$$

A total of 1,130 men were not in the army.

The peninsula's location in the Mediterranean Sea allowed Rome to easily reach other lands around the Mediterranean. The Romans came into contact with other Mediterranean peoples like the Greeks. The Greeks were a great influence on the Romans. Romans even began to worship Greek gods and goddesses. They gave these gods and goddesses Roman names and built temples to honor them.

This photograph shows the ruins of ancient Roman temples built to honor the Roman gods Jupiter and Juno. Jupiter was king of the gods and was based on the Greek god Zeus. Juno was queen of the gods and was based on the Greek goddess Hera.

Although the Roman Republic was established in 509 B.C., it took hundreds of years for a truly republican government to develop. In the early years of the republic, only landowning members of the upper class—called patricians (puh-TRIH-shunz)—were allowed to hold political office, interpret law, or become priests. Members of the lower class—called plebians (plih-BEE-uhnz)—had few rights. They fought to hold government positions during the 400s and 300s B.C. Around 287 B.C., plebians had gained political equality but great differences between the two classes still remained.

Around 280 B.C., most of the Italian peninsula was under Roman control. During the 200s and 100s B.C., Roman rule gradually spread to large areas of land overseas. During this period, Rome fought several battles with Carthage, a city on North Africa's Mediterranean coast that served as a large trading center. These battles were called the Punic Wars. Rome destroyed Carthage in 146 B.C., gaining control of the Mediterranean coasts of Africa and Spain. Let's say that during one battle of the Punic Wars, the total number of Roman soldiers and Carthaginian soldiers who died in battle was 783. If 231 of those who died were Roman soldiers, how many soldiers from Carthage died? Look at the math box below to see how to set this up as an algebraic equation.

$$x + 231 = 783$$
$$x + 231 - 231 = 783 - 231$$
$$x = 552$$

Of the soldiers who died in the battle, 552 were from Carthage.

This scene of the Punic Wars, painted in the early 1500s, shows Rome's victory over Sicily, an island located off the southern tip of the Italian peninsula.

As the Punic Wars were ending, Rome's rule was spreading to eastern lands. By the mid-100s B.C., Rome had conquered both Macedonia and Greece and controlled part of Turkey. Despite the republic's victories overseas, there were problems back in Rome. During the Punic Wars, the farmlands and houses of Roman farmers had been destroyed. Farm families crowded into the cities, seeking work. Wealthy patricians bought the farmlands and brought slaves from conquered lands to work on them. Slaves also filled many jobs in cities. Unemployed farmers grew angry and desperate. Leaders of the republic disagreed on how to stop the growing unrest, and the republic grew weaker.

In the 60s B.C., Roman rule again spread overseas to eastern lands like Syria and Asia Minor. During the 50s B.C., a Roman general named Julius Caesar conquered Gaul, a large area made up of modern-day France, Belgium, and Switzerland, plus parts of Germany and the Netherlands. By 48 B.C., Caesar ruled the Roman Republic. Four years later, Caesar was killed by political opponents who feared his power. Octavian (ahk-TAY-vee-uhn), Caesar's grandnephew and heir, became the first Roman emperor in 27 B.C., and the Roman Empire was born.

During the Roman Empire's peak, its capital city of Rome had the largest population of any city in the empire. It is estimated that the empire's next largest city, Alexandria in Egypt, had 750,000 people. Some experts believe this was about 250,000 fewer people than Rome had. How many people lived in Rome? Look at page 23 to see how we can set this up as an algebraic equation.

When Octavian became emperor in 27 B.C., he took the name Augustus, which means "revered one." His reign began a long period of peace in the Roman Empire that lasted for about 200 years.

In this equation, x represents the number of people living in Rome during the Roman Empire's peak. Since we know the population of Alexandria (750,000) was 250,000 less than the population of Rome, we can set the equation up as follows:

$$x - 250,000 = 750,000$$
$$x - 250,000 + 250,000 = 750,000 + 250,000$$
$$x = 1,000,000$$

About 1,000,000 people lived in Rome during the peak of the Roman Empire.

23

The Empire Prospers

Under the rule of Augustus, the empire's government became more stable. The Roman Empire thrived for many years. After Augustus died in A.D. 14, a line of his **descendants** ruled the Roman Empire, which reached its height of power and wealth between about A.D. 96 and A.D. 180. Though the empire did not grow much larger after Augustus's death, new towns and cities were established, and a network of roads was built that allowed distant places to communicate with the rest of the empire more easily.

Roman literature and art also reached a high point during this period. Roman writers and artists borrowed from Greek traditions for much of their work. Writers were influenced by Greek drama and poetry. Painters created large works showing figures from Roman **mythology**, which was based on Greek mythology. Sculptors used Greek ideas about the human form in the statues and carvings they created, which were used to decorate buildings and monuments throughout the empire.

Let's say that one Roman sculptor created a total of 47 works during this period. Along with a second sculptor, the 2 artists created a total of 98 works. How many works did the second sculptor create? We can set this up as an algebraic equation.

$$x + 47 = 98$$
$$x + 47 - 47 = 98 - 47$$
$$x = 51$$

The second artist created 51 sculptures.

This image shows a detail from the Ara Pacis, or Altar of Peace. The Altar of Peace was created during the reign of Emperor Augustus as a symbol of the peace throughout the Roman Empire during his rule. The figures in the sculpture are shown wearing clothing of the period.

The Colosseum was built between A.D. 75 and A.D. 79, and was used for more than 400 years. Today, the ruins of the Colosseum still stand near the center of Rome.

Many impressive works of architecture were also created during this period. Again, the Romans borrowed from Greek architectural ideas and forms. As we saw previously in this book, the Romans built temples that were modeled on Greek temples, with central buildings surrounded by columns. The Romans often built much larger buildings than the Greeks had built, such as **amphitheaters** that could seat tens of thousands of people.

A building called the Colosseum (kah-luh-SEE-uhm) in Rome is the most famous Roman amphitheater and could hold about 50,000 people. People went to the Colosseum to watch men fight each other or hunt wild animals. This was considered a great source of entertainment. Ancient Romans also loved chariot races, which were held in large, oval-shaped arenas. Rome's largest arena may have seated up to about 5 times as many people as the Colosseum did. We can set this up as an algebraic equation.

x = people the largest arena seated
50,000 = people the Colosseum seated

$$x = 5 (50,000)$$
$$x = 250,000$$

Rome's largest arena could hold about 250,000 people!

Though Roman architecture was heavily influenced by the Greeks, the Romans created unique architectural features of their own. The Romans used curved structures called arches in many of their buildings. Arches can support great amounts of weight and allowed the Romans to build immense buildings and bridges. The Romans also used arches to build aqueducts. An aqueduct is a structure that carries water from one place to another.

The ancient Romans' use of aqueducts made it possible to keep the city of Rome well supplied with water. Around A.D. 100, 9 aqueducts brought an estimated 85,000,000 gallons of water a day to Rome from water sources in the mountains. If 2 of these aqueducts delivered a total of 18,000,000 gallons of water to Rome each day, and each of these 2 aqueducts delivered the same amount of water, how many gallons of water did each aqueduct deliver each day? Let's set this up as an algebraic equation.

x = **number of gallons of water 1 aqueduct carried**
$2x$ = **number of gallons of water 2 aqueducts carried**
$2x$ = **18,000,000**

We divide both sides of the equation by 2 to find out how many gallons of water 1 aqueduct carried.

$$\frac{2x}{2} = \frac{18,000,000}{2}$$

$$x = 9,000,000$$

Each aqueduct carried 9,000,000 gallons of water to Rome each day.

One of the most famous of the ancient Roman aqueducts is the Pont du Gard. This aqueduct still stands in southern France, which was

The End of an Empire

There were a number of reasons for the end of the Roman Empire. Its vast size, outside invaders, health and environmental issues, and internal problems led to its weakening and eventual collapse. By A.D. 476, the empire had completely broken down.

In this book we have read about the culture and civilizations of ancient Greece and Rome. We have learned how to express and solve problems using algebraic equations. Algebraic equations have helped us to understand and learn more about the ideas, insights, and accomplishments of the ancient Greeks and Romans and the influence these 2 civilizations have on the architecture, art, government, and literature we use and enjoy today.

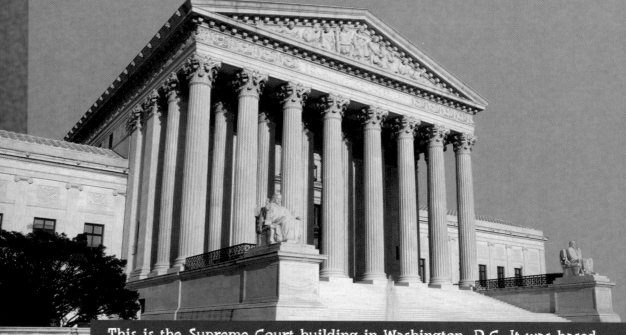

This is the Supreme Court building in Washington, D.C. It was based on Greek and Roman temples.

Glossary

acropolis (uh-KRAH-puh-luhs) The upper part of an ancient Greek city located on the top of a hill. The acropolis was enclosed by a wall to protect it from enemies.

amphitheater (AM-fuh-thee-uh-tuhr) A circular or oval building with rising rows of seats surrounding an open space in the center.

archaeologist (ar-kee-AH-luh-jist) A person who studies the people, customs, and life of the past.

architecture (AR-kuh-tek-chuhr) The science and art of designing buildings.

assembly (uh-SEM-blee) A branch of government made up of representatives elected by the people.

constant (KAHN-stunt) The name given to numbers in algebra problems, since they do not change.

descendant (dih-SEN-duhnt) Someone who comes from a particular ancestor.

equation (ih-KWAY-zhun) A statement that 2 quantities are equal.

mythology (mih-THAH-luh-jee) A collection of legends or stories that try to explain why things are the way they are.

peninsula (puh-NIHN-suh-luh) A piece of land that sticks out from a larger body of land and is surrounded by water on 3 sides.

philosophy (fuh-LAH-suh-fee) The study of knowledge and the value of things.

plague (PLAYG) A disease that spreads quickly from one person to another and usually causes death.

republic (rih-PUH-blik) A government in which the citizens elect people to manage the government.

variable (VAIR-ee-uh-buhl) In algebra problems, an unknown number represented by a letter.

Index